A FUN AND EASY WAY TO

GET GOOD GRADES

Written By Joy Berry
Illustrated by Bartholomew

Joy Berry Enterprises, Inc.
146 West 29th St., Suite 11RW
New York, NY 10001

Cover Design & Art Direction: John Bellaud
Art Production: Geoff Glisson
All music remastered at Midtown Sound Studios NYC, 2008

Printed in Mexico

ISBN 978-1-60577-311-7

To get good grades, you need to know
- the purpose of tests,
- the purpose of evaluations,
- what a high grade means,
- what a low grade means, and
- what you can do about low grades.

How do you feel when you are told to get good grades?

When you are told to get good grades, do you sometimes feel frustrated and confused?

When you think about grades, do you wonder. . .

If you follow the instructions outlined in this book, you can understand the purpose of grades and learn to use the information they provide to benefit yourself.

Spending time in school going over things you already know wastes time.

However, it is important that you not skip over things you need or want to know.

You and your teacher need to identify what you have and haven't learned. This is the only way to make sure that you don't
- waste time going over things you already know, or
- skip over things you need or want to know.

The best way to find out whether someone has or hasn't learned a subject is to **test** the person's knowledge of the subject.

A test usually involves asking the person questions about a subject to find out what he or she does or does not know about it.

There are **two kinds of tests.** One kind is a **verbal (oral)** test, in which the questions and answers are spoken.

Another kind of test is a **written test,** in which the answers to the questions are written.

The main purpose of a written or oral test is to find out what you have or have not learned about a subject.

If a test shows that you have learned certain information, you are ready to move on to new information.

If a test shows that you haven't learned certain information, you might want to review it until you have learned it.

A wrong answer on a test helps identify what you haven't yet learned.

Giving a wrong answer does *not* mean that you are
- unintelligent,
- lazy, or
- not as good as someone who knows the correct answers.

Some people who give wrong answers on tests might think of themselves as being unintelligent. They might also feel that they are lazy or are not as good as others. People who have these feelings about themselves might believe that, to be acceptable, they must know everything.

The truth is, no one person knows everything.

Even very old, very wise people do not know everything. There are always new things they can learn.

If the world's most intelligent people were tested on subjects they knew nothing about, the answers they would give to the questions asked probably would be wrong.

However, giving wrong answers would not mean that these people were unintelligent. Also, it would not mean that they were lazy or were not as good as people who could answer the questions correctly.

It would only mean that they didn't yet know the subjects on which they were tested.

A test is a way of finding out what you do and don't know about a subject. Therefore, you should not study a subject just because you are going to be tested on it.

You should not learn something so you can give the correct answers on a test.

Instead, you should learn a subject because it's something you need or want to learn. When you truly know a subject, you can easily answer any questions about it.

Just as tests help you realize what you do and don't know about a subject, **evaluations** help you realize how well you're learning the things you are expected to learn.

There are **two kinds of evaluations.** One is a **verbal evaluation,** in which another person tells you how well he or she thinks you are doing. Student-teacher conferences and parent-teacher conferences are verbal evaluations.

A second kind of evaluation is a **written evaluation,** in which another person explains in writing how well he or she thinks you are doing.

A note or letter your teacher writes about your work is a written evaluation.

Grades (sometimes called **marks**) are a kind of written evaluation. Grades are numbers or letters that indicate how well a student has learned what he or she is expected to learn.

There are many kinds of grades. Here are examples of letter grades and number grades and what they mean:

One kind of letter grade	What the grade means
A	excellent
B	very good
C	good
D	poor
F	failing

A second kind of letter grade	
E	excellent
S	satisfactory
N	needs improvement
U	unsatisfactory

One kind of number grade	
95 -100	excellent
90 - 94	very good
84 - 89	good
78 - 83	average
70 - 77	poor
below 70	fail

A plus sign beside a letter or number or grade means that the quality of the student's work is between one grade and the next higher one. For example, a B+ is between a B and an A.

A minus sign beside a letter or number or grade means that the quality of the student's work is between one grade and the next lower one. For example, a B- is between a B and a C.

The plus or minus indicates what grade the student's work is closer to. For example, a B+ is higher than a B but lower than an A-, and a B- is lower than a B but higher than a C+.

If you receive a high grade, it's probably because you have learned a subject well.

Receiving a high grade does not mean that you are
- more intelligent,
- less lazy, or
- more acceptable

than someone who received a lower grade than you.

If you receive a low grade, it most likely indicates that you did not learn something you were expected to learn.

Receiving a low grade does not mean that you are
- unintelligent,
- lazy, or
- not as good as someone who received a higher grade than you.

There could be several reasons that you might not learn something you were expected to learn.

One reason could be that **you have personal problems.** These problems might make it impossible for you to concentrate on your schoolwork.

Another reason you might not learn something you are expected to learn is that **you aren't ready to learn it.** The subject might be too difficult for you to understand.

If you haven't learned something that you are expected to learn, it might be because **you don't care** whether or not you learn the subject. Maybe you aren't interested in the subject, or maybe you aren't convinced it is something you need to learn.

Another reason you might not learn something is that **the subject isn't being presented properly.** Maybe it isn't being taught in a way that you can understand or in a manner that makes you want to learn it.

When you receive a low grade, there's always a reason. It's important that you, your parents, and your teacher do two things:

1. Determine the reason for the low grade.

2. Do something about it.

Once you find out why you haven't learned what you were expected to learn, there are several positive things you can do about the situation.

You might find out that you haven't been able to learn because **your attention has been on your personal problems,** not on your schoolwork.

If you are like most people, schoolwork is easier for you when your personal problems are not getting in the way of your learning.

To improve the situation, there are several things you can do:

- Spend some time and energy dealing with your problems.
- If necessary, ask a caring adult (a parent, teacher, or counselor) to help you work on your problems.

Once you resolve your problems, you can give your full attention to your schoolwork.

You might find out you haven't been able to learn because **you weren't ready to learn the subject** or because **it was too difficult for you to understand.**

To improve the situation, there are several things you can do:

- Talk to your parents. Ask them to work with you to help you learn the subject.
- Talk to your teacher and ask him or her to explain the subject to you until you understand it.
- If talking to your teacher doesn't work, ask someone else to work with you until you understand the subject. The person you ask to help can be a friend, relative, or tutor.
- If working with someone else doesn't work, ask your teacher to allow you to work on other subjects until you are ready to try again. You might try again after a week, a month, or several months have passed. Your teacher can help you decide how long you should wait before working on the subject again.

You might find out that you haven't been able to learn because **you're not interested** in the subject or because **you're not convinced** that you need to learn it.

To improve the situation, there are several things you can do:

- Talk to your parents. Ask them to tell you why it's important for you to learn the subject.
- If your parents don't know why it's important for you to learn the subject or if you aren't satisfied with their answer, talk to your teacher. Ask him or her to explain why learning this subject is important.
- If your teacher doesn't know why it's important for you to learn the subject or if you aren't satisfied with his or her answer, talk to your principal or to the curriculum director in your school district (the person responsible for the courses of study for the schools).

Talking to your parents, teacher, principal, and district curriculum director might help you see the importance of studying a particular subject. Understanding why a subject is important might make you want to learn it.

However, even if you still aren't convinced that you need to learn the subject, talking to adults about how you feel can be helpful. It might cause them to consider whether learning the subject is truly important. The questions you ask possibly might influence them to make a needed change in the curriculum.

Of course, you may never be satisfied with the answers you receive about why you need to learn a particular subject. If this happens, you need to do the best you can in the situation.

You might find out that you have not been able to learn because the **subject was not presented properly** or was not taught in a way that motivated you to learn.

To improve the situation, there are several things you can do:

- Talk to your teacher about it. Politely explain how you feel and suggest what he or she could do to change the situation. You might even offer to help your teacher with special projects to make learning the subject more interesting.
- Study the subject outside of school. Ask your parents, friends, relatives, or people such as librarians to help you. Together, you might be able to approach the subject in an entirely new, exciting way.

It is important to keep in mind that some people blame everyone but themselves for their low grades. Often they are not willing to do what they must do to learn a subject.

Remember, no one can learn for you! You must learn for yourself! So, before you blame your teacher or someone else when you haven't learned something, ask yourself this question:

"Am I doing everything I can do to learn what I am expected to learn?"

Knowing the purpose of grades and using the information they provide can benefit you in many ways.